THE WILD PUPIL

First published in 2012
by Bradshaw Books
Tigh Filí, Civic Trust House, 50 Pope's Quay, Cork
www.bradshawbooks.com

ISBN: 978-1-905374-32-8

Front cover image taken from *Grant's Atlas of Anatomy*, reproduced
courtesy of Lippincott Williams & Wilkins.

Cover design and typesetting by Jamie O'Connell.
Author headshot (back cover): Brendan Harrington.

10 9 8 7 6 5 4 3 2 1

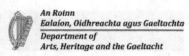

THE WILD PUPIL

Kathy D'Arcy

bradshaw books

Acknowledgements

Acknowledgements and thanks are due to the following: the editors of *Southword*, in which 'Plums' first appeared, Maire and the team at Bradshaw Books, Jamie O'Connell for invaluable help and advice, and Denis Greig and all at Lapwing Publications. To my writing students, thank you for your honesty and inspiration. Finally, thanks to Declan.

Contents

For Mona

First Furniture

I'm sorry about
the trail of hair I leave
on every surface, lapping at the edges
of the bed, the toilet –
I'm shedding my old life,
will soon be shinily bald with possibility.

Plums

They give me plums,
but I leave them aside;
I leave them alone
until
they fill and darken
and swell,
a sweetness this side of wrong,
and then
I accept them
one by slithering one
into my mouth,
licking the liquid flesh from the bones,
collecting the stones.

Work

After you leave
I follow the trail of you around the house
with the Hoover.

You wandered into my kitchen,
my bedroom, my good room,
picking things up
while you were meant to be working,

lost a hammer, a spirit level, a hacksaw
in the soft insulation of my attic.

Body Parts

Use my fingers
Blend coral into my lips

The tight cage shakes
Before the blade.

Christmas

Brushing wet hair,
so much comes away
that I throw it
routinely
into the fire.
It hisses up the chimney.

Passenger

She sits in the front seat
while he scrapes
with his credit card.

Arranges her face.
Expressions get tired,
are replaced.

Her lips stuck together.

He alternates;
rhythmic, frantic.

No matter what, it appears,
he is getting her home.

Bone White

He is made of water,
I know now —
beneath the icy surface of his skin
like Jupiter's moon.

When you land on him
he turns sparkle-coated,
afloat unwittingly,
scattering the vacuum

with mists
that varnish the sun,
rinse the sky,

waves
that knock trees together,
shear the rock layer
off mountains,
boil out of rivers,
asphyxiating —

washed bone white.

Hen

No eggs for weeks,
and I know about
the complex grotesque of the vent,
the scrolls of frustrated eggmaking;

ultrasound clouds
of variously blistered-off baubles
around hiccuping, adolescent ovaries.

When we turned her into the hole
we weren't quick enough to escape
a glimpse.

Coil

One sharp tug.
It was out.

My body contracted.
She held up the squirming thing,
filmy with blood
as though living.

Beginning

I wander, pick up
something called a bath bomb;
you will need to patch an uneasy truce
with your sullen body after this.

A scented bath, the imminent explosion.
You are changing into somebody else.

The Dresser

My pregnant sister
clears out the dresser:
forgotten presents on the dusty top,
coats for fancy parties,
spiders;
books about marriage, children, love
on the second; books *for* children,
management books on the third, Guinness
Books of Records;

fourth shelf adult nappies,
first aid kits, deodorants, antibacterial wipes,
plasters; the bottom presses not opened.

She works her way up
using the wipes,
sweeps the rest into refuse sacks.

On a chair in the end,
Pledge-soaked rag in hand, she finds
an old picture of the dresser.
Bare, newly cleaned.

Tomorrow, our mother
will come upon Enid Blyton books
she thought she threw out years ago,
will arrange them on
the third shelf.

The Way

We gathered them to the fire,
left them on rocking chairs –
had nothing to say to them.

In the awkward silence after the rain
we reflected that nobody likes to get wet.

Good China

My cousins and I
raffled
the tea-sets
left over
when the house
was empty.

I got the one I wanted.
It's in the top press,
waiting
to be broken.

Comfort

The liquid
in the kitchen

I knew was bad, but
couldn't
not
drink;

I was made sick,

do not remember the taste,
but long for the blue,
the yellow,
the pink.

Mystery

Banging behind the Sacred Heart,
the prayer for the precious family
in the dark hallway.

Cards falling
from their niches in the frame.
Light flickering.
Is that you on the roof?

Looking down
at the empty driveway,
across the valley,
over the side,
the gaping patio,
rush of the tiles —

My bed is hot and delicious.
I'll check in the garden later.

I've cleaned the filth off my fingernails,
I've shoveled back in my entrails;

glorious.

First Rose

Otherworldly thorns at the end
of the second bouquet —
a rose.

It died slowly
in a pint glass by the sink,

went in the compost bin,
and is still there,

not composting.
Not real enough
to help anything grow.

Courgette

I live beside
the maternity hospital
and receive a box of food
each week.

You buy me vegetables.
Courgettes.
I wonder if you know what they are;
if you think I'll know.

Love

I'm transcribing your texts
into my computer
at three in the morning.

Christmas II

The bath is full.
The water outside
is frozen to a depth of inches.

I shower, having encountered the
bathtub.
Warm water courses, excessive, luxurious,
over my face
and will not stop.

Heartworm

Dogs can get 'heartworm' –
I saw a sign in the vet's.

Like *fasciola hepatica* maybe, all
suckers and hermaphroditism, slithering
through myriad nebulous stages,
leaving a trail of
tentacles and fractalated slime.

Their hearts full of them,
walls straining with coronary elephantiasis.

How would you get them out.

The Line

Feral kittens out the back
you say,
preparing milk.

But I'll be staying here,
not taking the bait,

while you bring your gift outside
and wait.

The Wild Pupil

I have spent my life
squeezing my fingers between
vibrating leaves of costal bone,
insistently scraping fascia
from muscle from nerve,
unhooking your sternum
from your throat,
prizing apart
the wedges of your spine

to reach that precious bag of blood,
to quell its chaotic pulse;

to jump back
as your thorax springs open
like an eye,
your heart
the wild pupil.

Exploration

Pulling gently
a fibrous thread
out of the nail bed
of my little toe,
I neatly unravel.

Hospit

The walls are flaking,
wiped off vomit:
harpicked wheezes, catheters,
bedpans, surgical drains.

They creep
through wards,
their greenish nails
easing paint off.
Staring,
their skin flaking –
relentless wiping.

Inside III: Procedure

A small cut made in the groin;
the stiff line fed in;
the patiently poking progress
up the intimate centre
to the heart, glowing blue on the screen.

The switch thrown,
the flash,

the dizzying syncopator
of fibrillation
cauterised.

Back to the dull thud.

Burned

First time in theatre
they wheel him in;

black-pink blotches,
piglet noises,
small swollen limbs.

The Dermatome
scrapes off remaining skin,
to wrap around fingers,
torso, cheeks.

Some cry; I
watch
behind my mask.

Tight black scrap.
By now you have been
patched and stitched,
a writhing map.

Two Verses

A nauseating crack on the crown;
flesh pinched between fingernails;
slowly pulling detached skin away;
rooting a thorn out with a pin.

A nightmare's enforced paralysis;
ridicule from hidden shadows;
knowing the suffering of animals;
the thorn staying in.

Forensics

No body
however evil its smell
and appearance
is ever so autolysed
as to render an autopsy
unnecessary (on the
contrary, the need
for a careful autopsy
becomes greater in these
circumstances).

Probable Misuse of Shamenism

I clamber through your Great Vein
(or Inferior Vena Cava,
as it is properly known).
Surrounded by black, stagnant blood, and
the beat of the drum, if I work
hard enough I will come
to the writhing bowl of your Right Atrium,
and then the possibilities are endless.

I can sit quite still, with a choking gutful
of irony wine, and allow
my foreign-ness to disrupt the smooth flow
(Turbulence, that is called)
through the Mitral Valve, so that
little clots form and are shot around and out
to your lungs;
an exercise in anticipation for me, the knowing wait
for the sharp pain, the breathless death.

I can kick and claw at the great central wall
to make a small hole, and squeeze through
to the business side; from there
I will have no choice
but to be shunted straight to your brain,
whence a dullness will spread
and the 'F-A-S-T' protocol from the stroke ads
will come into play.
Then, like that old film, I will have to exit through
the nearest opening (your rheumy eye probably) before
I run out of 'T for Time'.

I can simply tear it apart –
though this would be most difficult, it feels
the most satisfying –
begin with cutting the beautiful strings,
then rip off the valve-lips like so many yogurt lids,
finally work my hands bloody
(like crying in a swimming pool)
taking the central divide asunder;
yes, how satisfying to gut it like that, so
nothing can hide!

Sometimes I feel so much strength
that I think I could reach in under
your straining ribcage with my bare hand
and pluck the grotesque, pulsating thing out
like a weed;
but they beat independently, and
I can't imagine not flinging it away in disgust,
not screaming and stamping like a child with
an eel, not cowering in a corner while
the pathetic lump convulses its last.

The book says to make sure and come out
before the drum-beat stops;
I'm not sure what happens otherwise.

Flytrap

Gentle, curious pressure
will pull a nail from its root,
a tooth from its head
in time.

Holes

Two syringes attached to a three-way valve,
antecubital insertion in the left arm,
ten mls of solution agitated to make bubbles.

I push the mixture up them.
It fills one side of the heart onscreen,
milling in the chambers like static.

I wait to see
if there are holes.

Mona

I made cuts along the white of your forearm.
We pulled it apart – a diamond
of linear tendons appeared.
We unwrapped the gauze from your face
and laughingly christened you Mona Lisa.

Sleep Deprivation

Hospital canteen,
dark acidic tea,
wet umbrella, empty
stomach.

I've eaten a raw tomato
like a sweet.

The curtain is broken, slaps
across speckled formica,
murals of Pluto the Dog,
and people who occasionally pass.

Night Duty

4am, aroused
by sleeping men
in paisley pyjamas,
yellow-pillow-half-smothered,
who sound like boys
I've taken home;
another night
of analgesic sleep.

Inside II: Terminology

I remembered about *Chordae Tendineae*
when a book fell open on a picture
of the straining threads.

They are strung inside
like thick pink parallel fronds of spit,
holding sides and walls together.

I thought about climbing in.

Inside

Behind the wood screens
neat hammers hang
tensed in tight arrays, ready
at easy bidding
to leap to the sounding-strings

in mocking cacophony.

I think about climbing inside,
touching the dark wooden guts,
tangling the careful sinews
around my half-developed parts;
its slave.

Placenta

He walked in,
rolled up his sleeve,
delivered the baby,
put his arm in,
retrieved the placenta,
drawing slowly
out.

She looked at her husband

with strange supine serenity,
hardly noticing.

You tilted your glass, spilled red wine on your arm,
purpled the skin, blackened the blonde hair.
Useless.

Keeping Your Mouth Closed

This rictus crackles
wrinkles in my shell
as if I'd been hit
with the spoon.

I let it expand.
A clawed baby foot
forces out of my mouth.

The slim air-sac inside
shrinks and crumples,
imploding the skin of my face.

It will walk first
on eggshells.

The Knife Sharpener

He only ever
drew our shrieking knives
through the sharpener
and filled up the fireplace
with our newspaper.

Sly-eyed in the drawer
after, the knives praised
the cauterising
usefulness of the fire.

Picture of You

I drew a picture of you
on the back of some old notes
and found, turning it around,
that the other side said Heart Disease.

Curse

He sits by the window
with an arm around her,
I'm so content, he says.

She makes stew,
they drink tea,
go to bed,
watch the 'Late Late',
he reads out the news.

Some morning
he'll have cataracts
and wrinkles,
sunken eyes,
a receding hairline;
her breasts will have deflated,
her cellulite spread;
they'll both be a little deaf,
and (God willing)
incontinent.

Cautery

I will burn the pages,
inserting the poker
between each one
in turn
so that orange mouthfuls
haemorrhage into the gaps.

I will scatter the razed black petals
(still crimson-edged)
to the stove's four corners.

Grief

When they told me
he was dead
I bought a flat-pack filing cabinet
with no instructions
and set to building it.

Hours later,
inside it,
palms bleeding,
I laughed.

What a relief
to hammer nails into
anything.

Or Metamorphosis

I used to heat the house
when I came;
now the breath that comes out of my mouth
cools my face.

Hypnopompic Finding of Oneself

At the bottom of the white-tiled pool
the wayward plaster of the future lurks,
a thin film of slimy potential
sticking it repeatedly to my foot.

Yellow

There's money to
plant them but not
to water them,
they just burn.

Up at dawn several days,
I walk alongside the rise

of acres of blackened faces
to the sun,

and witness also
the joyful wait
of the yellow young.

Lost World

Strange lesions
on our smooth upper arms.
We are *intoxicado*,
says the doctor in the sundress.

Drugged and dreaming,
I see through the vine-green ceiling
a plateau from the lost world,

straddle it,
a foot either side
in the bath-warm sea.
Like eyelashes, clouds and birds tickle my face.

Two Days' Absence

Now you are away,
my nakedness is merely
an unimportant result
of taking my clothes off.

Photograph

You stood behind me,
grazed your palm.

A tap,
a smack,
rock to the balls, the heels,
flash.

I warned you.

Back set in clean, straight lines,
a cold inch between torsos,
you suddenly take my hand
as if we were married.

Flying

I swoop over the car park of my old school,
the pattern visible in my mind,
a work of art.

Chain

A dark blue chain oozes from my pen;
I lift it and set it in my hair.

People start.
Miraculous grace, my ink-wet crown
leaks down my face like thick
blue eyeliner.

Run

People run past in the afternoon,
I have worked all night.

I run past houses
out late,
footfalls echoing.

We think
the city is full of tearing, ecstatic feet.

Days

You left me spread sideways
the first day,
opening and closing my fists.

My newborn godson had learned,
the second day,
the fat contentment of just being alive.